STRANGER'S NOTEBOOK

STRANGER'S NOTEBOOK

Poems

NOMI STONE

TriQuarterly Books
Northwestern University Press
Evanston, Illinois

TriQuarterly Books
Northwestern University Press
www.nupress.northwestern.edu

Printed in the United States of America

10 9 8 7 6 5 4 3 2 1

Library of Congress Cataloging-in-Publication Data

Stone, Nomi.
Stranger's notebook / Nomi Stone.
p. cm.
Includes bibliographical references.
ISBN 978-0-8101-2509-4 (cloth : alk. paper) — ISBN 978-0-8101-2510-0 (pbk. : alk. paper)
1. Jews—Tunisia—Jarbah Island—Poetry. I. Title.
PS3619.T665S77 2008
811.6—dc22

2008019600

∞ The paper used in this publication meets the minimum requirements of the American National Standard for Information Sciences—Permanence of Paper for Printed Library Materials, ANSI Z39.48-1992.

These poems are dedicated to Alite Bitane of the Hara Kebira.

They are also for my sister, Lia, and my brother, Zach.

Among countless stones, one stone becomes sacred—
and hence instantly becomes saturated with being.

—MIRCEA ELIADE

The Jewish community on the island of Djerba, off the coast of Tunisia, might have arrived in North Africa after the fall of Jerusalem's First Temple, in 586 B.C.E. According to myth, a handful of exiles—Kohanite Jews, of the priestly caste—arrived on the island carrying a single stone from the destroyed holy place. The community believes that the stone is still lodged in the frame of their largest synagogue, called La Ghriba, or "The Stranger." Many Djerbans tell that the temple is named after an anonymous young girl who arrived alone to the island. When the girl's isolated hut spontaneously burned, she was named a saint, and the synagogue was erected over the sanctified spot. Djerban Judaism is especially inflected with messianism: a better age, a return to a perfect era, is expected to occur one day, starting in Jerusalem. Mourning the fall of the Temple and seeking to repair it and the torn cosmos through community and prayer are deeply a part of the Djerban Jewish cosmology.

This diminishing pocket of Jews lives, largely peacefully, in the midst of the Arab world. Their village is called the Hara Kebira ("Large Quarter") and has historically been inhabited only by Jews. Although their enclosure is not demarcated by a physical barrier, it is felt and perhaps created both by the community itself and by the surrounding Muslim communities. In the last fifty years, 80 percent of the Djerban Jews have emigrated to France and Israel, but the thousand remaining live with piety and a protective and rejoicing inwardness. Most of the men are silver workers, like their fathers and grandfathers before them. The women marry young and raise their children to be proud of their heritage and wary of outsiders. Their world is steeped in ritual and orthodoxy; its crystalline preservation is surely a product of their historical insularity. Every child in the community learns Hebrew, though the local Arabic dialect is spoken in the homes. The Sabbath is observed meticulously. The Torah, the holy book, is perceived as the ultimate source of wisdom and fulfillment; the Zohar, a Jewish mystical text, offers the community a paradigm of eventual messianic redemption after exile. These practices and beliefs coexist, sometimes uneasily, with satellite televisions—broadcasting Israeli news or reality shows—in a fair number of Djerban Jewish homes. In the sixty years since the creation of Israel, the community's relationship with the surrounding Muslim communities, once much more permeable, has become increasingly difficult. This rupture is certainly born of modern politics, as the two communities have coexisted for centuries, and perhaps millennia.

In 2002, al-Qaeda bombed the synagogue, killing eighteen European visitors and causing some structural damage, and this remote Jewish community was briefly thrust into Western consciousness—and irreversibly into my own. I lived in the community (initially on its peripheries and eventually in the center of the town) during part of 2003 and 2004. *Stranger's Notebook* is written from the edge of that sacred circle. The last section of the collection was written after I spent several weeks in Israel interviewing Djerban emigrants during the 2005 Gaza withdrawal. Most had come to Israel just after the state was established in 1948.

CONTENTS

IV

V

VI

STRANGER'S NOTEBOOK

Beginnings

In a myth that came before
the myths by which we now live,
the Earth and Sky halved when the boy-
god's arrow sent through his
grandmother's mouth reached
her heart.

1

The Stranger, Preparing for a Long Journey, 2003

Bring your yellow backpack, your
blank books, enough to remind you of
yourself. There will be thickets of
honeysuckle; tourists; people who
stayed. You have never seen
this island. But it is like an itch.
A whiff. Someone else's memory came
in.

The Fall of the First Temple, 586 B.C.E., *Jerusalem*

The priests buzzed around the nothing
that was left there, inspecting it with
itching fingers. One threw the useless
keys into the everything above. Now,

they must learn to make
a meadow a temple, an act or an absence of
an act, a temple. Weeping, they become
their altar.

Notes on How They Came

Some claim that the island is the continental drift of Palestine itself.

1. Arriving in Djerba, 586 B.C.E.

Those who still have not left here
Remember that millennia ago,
They carried a perfect white
Boulder from the broken edifice of their first
Country across to the top edge of
This African continent.

2. (Arriving in Djerba

Berbers,
Jews,
Phoenicians,
Romans,
Vandals,
Byzantines,
Arabs,
Spaniards,
Turks,
French,
Arabs)

3. Still Arriving

A recipe: *Basisa.* Comes from the word
asas, which means foundation, the foundation
of the broken edifice. You make it
with sugar and pounded wheat and oil. You close
the door to your home, because this moment
is secret, precious, private. You
stir it with a great key. You do not
invite anyone in.

La Ghriba ("The Stranger") Tells How and Why

The people who live here
do two things: their faces whiten past you or blacken into
you. Girls are not supposed to come to islands
by themselves; did no one tell you? You found

the highest hill, away from their whistles,
their eyes. Up here only windy grass, the blow of sea that brought you.
Only a few cigarette butts, pistachio shells. They come here,
but hardly. The house you make

is sticks and burrs. Dirt on white knuckles. The sea
through the cracks. They do not talk to you anymore, or look at you,
your first wish. The wind and sea are full of stomachs:
now, learn to disappear

into them. Your house's slender frame catches
fire one day. You hear them buzzing below. They watch,
they stand, wild brightness from the hill reflecting
in each eye. Light. Birds almost green among

the sparks. Is it the sun? No, the moon
has caught the sun in its mouth. The moon is nothing but the sun letting
it see itself. The question comes again, do you have too much faith
in people, or too little? Like when you were sitting on the ledge by the sea

and three large boys' shadows stubbed the grass.
Your first thought was, so they will make me fall. But they don't
make you fall. Whether they are afraid of you or you of them, whether
they are jeering, is not clear.

This is the island with the hill with the house with the girl with the fire
inside. Afterwards they climb to the top to look at something ruined
close-up. They touch the door, soft with ash:

the body, amongst the branches and birds,
is white. The face catches the sun's
light.

Jerusalem

The stones are tunnels
of light. The city touches
your funny bone with
a mallet of light, the feeling
of emerging from
a tunnel into a bright room.

They call this city
the navel of
the world. Once the cord
was snipped,
it bucked out of God's arms.

End of Time

When the sky's throat slit open, you saw
for the first time constellations
behind those you knew. Meanwhile, as usual,
a people keeps scattering, their libraries
burning. When you ask them,
they explain they simply want to be

on a single solid ground, no one forgotten or
lost. Living in this place together must be,
they imagine, the closest thing to the heavens
and earth at last joining. And if in fact there is no
such place, then plant them deep
inside what the sky might allow.

11

From Her Notes: The Village

This dusty rooster
announces dawn every white
quarter of an hour.

Milky green eyes scan
objects. This jeweler says no
to all things not whole.

Most say there are two
poor people here, and they eat
free wedding peanuts.

Whose daughter are you?
Whose daughter are you whose daugh-
ter are you whose daughter are—

My sentences are
so full of elbows and knees.
Will they speak to me?

Bring the children sweets.
They will invite you inside
soon.

Trapped on Djerba, Island of the Lotus Eaters

You are walking through a long grove. Pebbly sand underfoot. On the edge, a field
of colossal flowers, sagging low with pollen. Have you been here before, you think?

The sky phosphoresces, broken triangles between branches and stems.
Above you, gigantic pistils and stamens mingling in the cups of the flowers.
Ticks twitch in grass. You feel alive. Also wary.

No one stops you when you climb inside those white necks, breathe into
those white necks and lose all sense.   Like
a girl's belly, like the smell of her collarbone,

like—And what's more, the gulf was the same blue as the sky. We
(you were not alone) did not know which imitated which. Heavens stretched
out and up. Out, to that great sea roiling with histories. Up, implying
eternities. We lived equally between those blues. We still do.

"How to climb out of here?" asked one.

"Why?" answered another. Nothing exists
except what is one eyeblink below, one eyeblink above.

Day of Repentance, Day of Forgiveness

In the ten days in between the New Year and the Day of Repentance, the book is open: all creation hangs in balance between good and evil. Every individual act can make a distinct difference. On the Day of Repentance, the book closes.

Needle-thin insects under the vein
of leaf make the leaf breathe. One
is upside down opposite the other. Liquid

together. I watch, assume
they are making more of themselves. But instead,
one takes the other inside completely. One

perpetuates itself, which means the other
cannot. The yard is thick with trees, the trees
thick with this small drone.

The Girls

They drop a mandarin and a banana in your bag,
waiting for you at the door of the schoolhouse.
The girls are sixteen and not yet married. They giggle
their questions. "Whose daughter
are you?" "Why aren't you married yet?" They
know some words in your language; now and then
they say them. When you say words in theirs,
they peer at you and laugh and let you fumble until
you extract the right one, shining like
a bone they left for you many centuries ago in the sand.

First Day of School

Today the soft-eyed teacher gives the history lesson and the girls listen to the tale of their people. The memories we
are given to carry are (1) what was inflicted (2) whom to not trust.

We are sitting together on small benches in the classroom. One girl had beckoned to you to share her seat. They all
inspect your jewelry, your skirt, your waist. They want to know: "Do you like Britney

Spears?" and "What does your fiancé look like?" And in fact, you have fashioned a fiancé who would make your mother
proud. For now, he is in law school, has blue eyes, and is religious. But

because learning the intricacies of the law—those walls
beyond which one must not cross—is very difficult, he has so little time to call.

Learning Hebrew

Maybe they will learn to love me if I learn the biblical language. I learned it in my country too, but stumble awfully when I read, and besides the prayer words (Home, Peace, Land, Respect, Parents), only know the words for "watermelon" and "dog."

I must make diagrams in my notebook. The letter that sounds like *k* looks like a keyhole. The door firmly closed, but how the blue came through that opening as clean as a stab.

Learning Hebrew

You teach us English, they say, and we will teach you Hebrew. They cluck their tongues disapprovingly: to have learned the language of the Others before learning your own, how peculiar. But if it is to become yours, it will be one letter at a time.

Later, in a café in the center of town (where no respectable girl of the village would go), you copy letters into your children's exercise book. Your shoulders covered, your skirt long, you write *aleph aleph aleph* in your book. The Muslim men's eyes flash.

Still later, bare-shouldered, with your book of poems and your head jangling with words in many languages, you sit on the other side of the island, opposite a gemmed pool, amidst the anonymous babble of tourists.

Welcome Party

You arrive at the wedding by yourself, into
a cluster of startled girls, who ask: "Did you come

by yourself?" They pass you a plate of salted beans,
and when you smile at them warmly, they look back,

oddly moved, then return to their
chattering. Men dance. Women

tap heels under chairs. Their bright lips,
bright eyes, rings signal back and forth.

Plates of sweets are circulating around the room, then
suddenly, so is your notebook. It passes between

flashing rings. Teeth, laughing.
Beating drums. Pink lights over the bride's chair.

A girl at last hands back your book. On the last page, each
has carefully written her name, in their language, then in your own.

This House

Shame is, by nature, recognition.
I recognize that I am as the Other sees me.
—SARTRE

1

This is not your house. To whom do you belong to whom do you belong to whom
do you belong to whom do you belong to whom do you

2

This is her house and her face is cold. She is on her hands and knees on the dusty
turquoise tiles of this house you have been living in for a week.

Her son rented it to you without her permission and she wants to know who you think
you are.

She is on her hands and knees in the bathroom. You don't breathe, not fully existing as
you

watch her arms deep in the clogged toilet, the furious motion of her arms.
Out come tissues, smeared red, reminding you both: you are a girl with a body. And you

are a girl with no husband, no father, no
anyone but your self, its quiet loudness in this village, this house.

The window grill shadows a forest over both
your faces.

The neighbor enters without knocking, eyes troubled. She asks you (she) what is wrong.

What We Ask the Messiah to Save

When God was about to create man, both above and below,
all creatures commenced to tremble.
—ZOHAR, HEBREW BOOK OF MYSTICISM

"The moment my feet are on the stones of that land, I begin
Breathing," she tells me as the sun breaks
Red like a capillary on the sea. "Empty
My house my life. Leave me my land."

Learned men describe a great flame. Think of
Thinking of it—imagining it directly is too much
For normal souls like us. Changing colors enclose its
Most secret light, which, at the beginning of time, broke into

Us. "When there is a death there," she tells me,
"My day is backwards. I drop things.
My grief falls in the soup.
I feed it to my children."

III

Us and Them

Words of Tunisian Jews, 2004

"We only have slight differences in customs, like how we slaughter animals. We share the same principles and traditions."

From Her Notes

An upright thimble
in each girl's heart. Careful now,
or lose your best friend.

The schoolteacher of
history cuts his orange.
Neat surgery.

Your neighbor asks you
what it is you want to learn.
What is it you lack?

She says only our
people own the truest
truth.

Holy days start just
when you first see the moon's
stab. It's the seeing.

Many Scientists Convert to Islam

Conversations with a Muslim friend

1

So, if you don't believe in full it means you don't
believe. Words tumble onto the rock. A book
happens.

Okay then tell me about heaven's beautiful
food and women. Who are these women?

My friend says, "This life is like a twenty-minute train ride."
He says, "I live inside my
faith more fully every day."

I am standing on soaked pavement outside
that majestic hotel in the center of town. Just before
dark, the birds come in a furious swoop like
hornets, stinging the sky to let in

what is on the other side.

2

Then the next life is equally
about the body, denied in the first?

"Do you know the Prophet knew the exact number of bones in the human
body? And why do you ask so many questions? You ask
more questions than you take in breaths of air."

The birds beat. They crumple in
rivers of sky. At the same time every day. Kierkegaard said that

every instant a man in despair is contracting it. My friend is not
in despair; I am not in despair.

3

Kierkegaard says there are three kinds of despair: despair
at not being conscious of having a self, despair at not being
willing to be oneself, and despair at willingness to be

oneself. Listen, the train. Why complain about
the seat, the air conditioner? Just do
your best until you arrive.

During Ramadan, I fasted a week. I went to the mosque.

My friend's uncle said:
"So you are becoming Muslim?" I said: "No." He said: "Shame
on you."

In the cold November current, there is a whirring of wings. Sometimes
they cloud into petals, sometimes they don't.

4

When the forehead presses to the earth, the blood moves
down. In the joining, the self lightens. You must count the three perfect
joints of each finger to keep time. Make no mistake, you leave the body only

through the body. The train ride. This quiet voice that is borrowed or my own.

Us and Them

"I would make love to one of our

whores before I
would fuck one of their
bourgeoisie." There was a proverb,

like this: Don't trust a   if
he becomes a   even though
he remains a   for

forty years. And the sister opposite
proverb: Don't trust a   even
though he has been in the grave

for forty years. It was a difficult day,
a bomb had spun open
a bus, and children

had been crushed down by
a machine. Each wondered if he was born
too soon, if later would have been better, if 40

+ 40 + 40 + 40

The Wound

The window grill makes forests across
white walls. Ten years ago, they
shuttered this house closed. The cold woman
(whose mother and niece had once
lived here) tells you now to leave this house.

There was a man—an outsider—came looking
for the girl to do what men want to do
to girls. She was not home at that hour. Instead
he found the old woman, washing dishes
in the kitchen. He panicked. She was pinned in
the corner, then pinned in the forest of his

dark decision. She tells you to leave this house. The dark
inside this house throbs around the body until
that body releases us back into the present.

A Prayer

I rent a room above the others, who practice the other
religion and eat the other food.

The girls are alarmed: "Aren't you afraid?" And refuse
to come inside.

I go to the school, watch one girl teach children how
to pray. At the noon

bell, she: "Where are you
eating now?" I: "I don't know yet!" She: "You're not

afraid?" then rushes home. When my neighbor sees
me in the street, she invites me in

for couscous in a blue dish. She anxiously reports
she heard from the girls that I don't know how
to pray.

Jewish New Year

Ghosts in our fingers, so
ghosts in the holiday bread.

IV

How We Recognized Our Longing

The married woman's second bed is behind
a hush of white closing
curtains.   Her dirty week and

the week after too,
she sleeps in this other
bed. She will become

new again in the baths.
But until that moment,
he will not touch

her. If she wants to give
him a glass of water,
she leaves it

on his night table. Half
of all time aches with
the gift of not,

its memory of.

Practicing Stoicism

The young mother twines your hair in braids: "No, don't leave yet, please just stay a little longer." She boasts to the neighbors, "The girl has breakfast with me every morning. She comes to my house every day." In the house, three children scream until she finally locks the door with them inside and paces the streets, her gaunt face wrapped in a lace shawl.

They tell you her husband does not like women. That he comes home late after playing dominoes with the boys in the café. That occasionally or often he hits her. Their children are screaming behind the door, you hear them. One first-century philosopher asks that you distinguish that which you can change from that which you cannot. If you live this way, in perfect stoic acceptance, you will "never suffer from any harm." Calm blue heat on these white houses every day.

Haram

I am going to the supermarket, and Orly, who is sixteen, is in charge. First, the cheapest soap rinse. Then, four new pairs of the cheapest nylons, which I will surely scrag to pieces in a week. Clutching my elbow, she says, "Do not talk to anyone. Just get your things and leave, fast. They do not like us." In the food section I am told I can only purchase these crackers in the yellow package. Everything else is *haram.* No yogurt, haram. No cookies, haram. None of these are kosher, she explains. I do not understand. But if you do not understand, sometimes better to continue pushing your cart. Orly continues the list. Pants: haram. Cafés: haram. Girls do not like boys, haram. The boy must initiate everything. Fact: sometimes I will fail, no matter how careful I am here. Fact: even despite this, I will be liked by some of them.

The primary, colloquial meaning of *haram* is "forbidden, taboo, prohibited." It also means "sacred, sacrosanct."

Parable

They want to know if I know
Tom Cruise and I want to know how to ask
if they are upset that a girl may not speak
to a boy until he makes her a woman.

The sun is glowing hard on dusty streets
and whiter homes. The fox asked the fish,
"Why not live on land if you fear the fisherman?"
In this example, they are the fish. Their holy book,
water.

From Her Notes

My last Sabbath,
I follow the girls, who sneak into
the wedding

tent, scattered with sun
flower seeds and remnants of
celebration. They

each stand up on a
table. Take a crushed beer can
as a microphone,

sing and move their
fifteen-year-old hips. I watch,
clap for them, until

a small face peers in
the door. A boy. His face white
with something. The door

slamming, his very small
fist holding it shut, having
found what was inside

wrong. Enough, I tell
him; enough! He leaves. The girls
dance again, but less

bold. Look: the boy
has come back, is looking you
hard in the eye, through

the crack of the door.
There, in his hand, a neon
plastic BB

gun. He does this for
his grandmother and for his
son.

Women and Men

One book says: "Every man is obliged to take
a wife, to increase and multiply." In this community—in many—
a girl may not be touched (her hand, no; her hair, no) until given

to a man. "He who does not fulfill his obligation is like
one who sheds blood and diminishes the human race."
Somewhere, right now,

on a bed behind a door, or on rocks spilled
into sea, a crying girl (in her first
pain or fulfillment) sings herself real.

From Her Notes

Your new friend warms your
coffee. You tell stories of
the birds on the cup.

She is in love with
her husband. You see it when
she watches him pray.

When you are ill, she
knocks. No one else had knocked;
you live above Muslims.

You give her your blue
necklace because you could
love her. Unstrange, this.

V

When the Messiah Did Not Come

R., headmistress of Jewish school in Tunisia for forty years

To begin, God contracted into
Otherness, making a space
divinity could not touch. This space

was marked for the universe and
allowed for goodness or
evil. This is why the War could

happen and this is also why we
survived. I left Poland
when I was sent to this country

by the rabbi of my village,
to start a new school. He called
it my mission. As in, the souls

we were given are learning how
to save these souls we were given.

Ways to Be Redeemed

Eve and Adam were created side to side. When their union
became perfect, they turned face-to-face,

and the upper world too (for a moment) was perfect. Every
time, their bodies brought the universe closer to what it had

originally been. That is what they are talking about
Saturday mornings, in their house of

God, that was almost shattered
by a bomb last spring. The walls make

continuous movements back into
one's self: blue green mustard patterns ajar, opening like

eyes on peacocks' tails.
One boy sings the morning

prayer in a clear, high voice in a minor key doubling back to
regain each lost chord. The losing happens

faster than the gathering. When a journalist
is told that photography is forbidden

inside the synagogue, she takes
a small tape recorder out of her purse, thinks, "There—

the sound will be enough; they'll know."
One Native American tribe thought the earth would

fall from the sky without their
songs. So they did not stop

singing.   My body and the bodies
it loves sing long into their dead end.

Saturday Twilight

At the last edge of
Sabbath, as the first
two stars puncture

open the sky, a girl is watching
her father rub wine
at the base of his skull. The last

bone, he explains to her.

Outside of Time

During the Sabbath you are in other time. You carry nothing
but your continuing

breath. Enter here, where
time is not

time, inside an alignment of the heavenly
and earthly worlds. The same happens when two bodies

join: the worlds rowing under each
skin climb into a zygote. Birth. And then no-time again

when the ram's horn
possesses your walled village. The men

blow the horn on each day of rest—

when you hear it, you stop
your breath and wish.

Listen. Your breath
held.

    And those stars
    behind the stars you recognize,

they stay.

The Sabbath

Today do nothing as
you usually do. Time is pooling
open. No sorrow in this blue
breathing air. Do not touch

the light; do not brush your hair;
do not even speak

of what binds you in the week.
You have come here to
learn to be like us, or
not. For now we each inhale our sweet

share of sky. We will not release it until
sundown.

Why I Came

Djerba, Tunisia

Under amber, the nearly lost
city: I dream myself
here, to enter how I imagine
we had once lived, until our cities
were paved over, stones
from our graves laid
in the new city's walls.

I came because, here,
amber flooded and
cooled over the homes, over
hands blessing candles inside.
And breath from the lost
cities kept moving in living
throats.

The Path of the Boy-God's Arrow

That arrow. Above us like a wasp. We
must keep learning our language. We must
marry ours, our girls always chosen
by our boys. They will make

a tight and holy circle where the outside
cannot touch. Within this light,
we daub wine on our eyelids, behind our necks,
to protect against

our deaths. For centuries we
have been eating food separate from the
others, have been speaking so the others cannot
completely understand; only we can understand

each other. Salt and air always arrived in sudden
pockets of wind. And how the arrow hovered, black
with accuracy. How every island knew itself
from its sea.

Purim, Spring Festival: How to Escape Massacres

Today, to celebrate not
being annihilated long ago, we
eat curly pastries shaped

like the persecutor's ears. Then, we hang and
burn him: dig a great pit and nail two great planks.
The paper doll stands for the man and how foolish

his face! His down-turned mustache,
the pointing nose, the ugly lips we drew
for him! How unlike our own

faces. Haman is his name, and next to him
his wife will dangle and 10 children, all
criminals, or at least they would grow

to be criminals, so we better take care of them
now. Trade plates of cakes, children. Eat.
Run. Breathe. Continue being alive, meaning,

as they teach you, exact your revenge.

Purim

Firecrackers! Louder
than rifles—cover your
ears with 1 hand! Throw
the next with the other hand!
(Do not look down.)

Purim

The fire! How large it gets!
The kids, running, feel heat
on their cheeks.

Purification Rite

It is the month between not being
obliterated (celebration #1) and being
delivered into the holy land (#2).
Ready yourselves. Scour

each home. Paint the walls white.
Mothers, how insistently you now wash
your daughters' faces, scrubbing them of
whatever the world tried

to leave there. Together you clear
the drawers of crumbs. Gently now, soon
the desert to cross, and thereafter,
that land with its promises.

Time Ends

Miracles are hungry. Stars open and shut across
Stratospheres. Stars open and

Djerban Folk Song

Sung by a wedding singer in Tunisian Arabic in Israel

"Ruhi hna . . . ma>a l-galut.
Yerushalayim 'twassalni
fi l'ghena wa l'biyut."

My soul is here . . . with exile.
Jerusalem, come to me
in the songs and in the homes.

VI

[Portraits of Women Who Left]

Negev, Israel

Arriving

I am walking across leaf-shaded sidewalks, past benches and broken pomegranates,
purple red on the ground, summer flies cartwheeling across.

> Now and then I knock on a door. "Tedoui bil Arabi?" I ask, using their verb,
> the special verb for *to speak* used on their island.

Finally, I am here, with my yellow backpack.
Inside: blank books, blank tapes, clean underwear.

> They still think I am strange, but this time,
> they get used to it fast.

Shoshana, her teeny face like a pumpkin left out too long, asks me in.

> She does not even ask where I am staying because she knows, and lays
> clean sheets on the cot without a question and with very kind and completely
> unstartled eyes.

Where

Sometimes they ask: "Where are you staying?"

And I say: "Well, yesterday I stayed with Shoshana, who sings
at weddings, and before that I stayed with Louisa."

And they want to know, "Well, where are you staying now?" But every day is
different.

Where

Dry riverbeds are thick with acacias. Once
there was a sea here. Now, pale oysters
are deep in the grass. The streets, named
for great men, are quiet. Chairs scrape
the sidewalk. Laundry blows under
the leaves.

Taking Notes

1. When did you come?
2. Why / and also how?
3. There? vs.
4. Here?
5. Who are you (now)?

"We sold and bought, we all met in the center."

"No. We had no problems with them when we were there."

"We were all girls. Many sisters. My father was very afraid for us."

"We made coffee under the trees. Fatima brought eggs."

"A committee brought us here and gave us a bed and chicken to eat."

"We read about it, all of us. We all had a picture of it. The last place."

Shlomite speaks of a place where the whole being bears fruit.

Dancing in Ashqelon

I go to the beach, bare
foot on grassy sand A city
by the sea, on the edge Salt
cricks the air Live coals, meat
crackles in circles Live

music the sky
hums, dives like a bee in
an orchid above Near me,
a girl Fluorescent lights on
off on her bare

shoulders, her lithe, her
skin There is a concert in the
city by the sea There will be
10,000 people Each mind imagines
a flame, a dark shake, tries to shake it,

to dance instead There is a city
beneath this city beneath this,
all by the sea A bomb would disappear
every.

A Map

At the end of the 19th beginning of the 20th century on the island, a rabbi sage was consulted and said: If a Jew hears a Muslim utter a blessing upon smelling fragrant herbs, he should second the blessing by uttering, "Amen!" Because they both believe and both want to praise.

In another theological quandary, the sage advised that when a Jew blessed kosher meat, he could add, without contradiction or interruption of his blessing, "Allahu Akbar" to make the meat equally fit for Muslim consumption.

Yaffit and I sit on the balcony. Green. Thorns.

Roosters pecking under clotheslines.

We open her wedding trousseau so she can try on her heavy anklets, the red silken brocade.

She has not opened it for twenty years, so I must try them on too.

We sit together, the dress rustling between.

We are a five-minute cab ride from the land which is being returned.
Do not speak
your politics, because they trust you for the first time. They grieve
the loss
of the land, because without the land, the Messiah will stumble.
His map will blow away.
Wind will carry it. They will not be good enough.

The Closest Thing

How did you learn to speak this way? Ouzi, come here: the girl speaks like Mama. Get Mama! Please will you have some more soda, let me get you something to eat—sit here, sit gently next to my mother. She will not know what to do.

The women crack sunflower seeds and play dominoes. On the tapes, later,
I hear: the swish of game pieces, a car horn. Their many
voices, rusty with laughter. Mine, listening.

They sing the song for the bride, and with a sudden turn, insert me into the song: Naomi, *la Roussa*! It will be a very beautiful day, they insist, brushing a stray tendril of hair from my cheek.

One leader has died and the other leader has had a stroke.
Their organs failed inside them. Everyone watches

these faces: distinct and resolute, brow and nose, hot pupils
soften into blankness.

In the Songs and in the Homes

I am sitting at a sunny table in Ohio with my sister. I tell her I have eaten pork and might eat it again. She does not understand. "Don't you feel connected to anything?" Lia, I have asked myself your question again and again: if you do not choose, is nothing yours?

"What is it you want to learn?" they asked me, "What is it you lack?"

Every night, the moon catches the sun in its mouth. You cannot see the moon otherwise.

The tape clicks. I turn over the tape.

We are by ourselves now. You are telling me your story and
I am listening, or it is the other way around.

Our chairs squeak, we shell seeds at the table,

until it is dark, and there, the first star.

ACKNOWLEDGMENTS AND NOTES

Thank you to the Fulbright Program, which enabled me to gather a year of fieldwork in Djerba in 2003 and 2004. My great appreciation also to Oxford University, which allowed me to hone and contextualize that fieldwork during the subsequent two years. The advice of Dr. Ronald Nettler, professor of Islamic thought, has been indispensable. Thank you also to Dr. Nadia Jamil and Nooman Kacem, who assisted me in questions of Arabic. Any fault in language or otherwise is my own.

My profound gratitude to Cleopatra Mathis and to Jorie Graham for their vision and for reading many drafts of these poems. Thank you to Lauren LeBlanc at Knopf for believing in the work of young poets. Thank you to my gifted editor, Mike Levine, and to all the staff at Northwestern University Press. Thank you to Lini, Holly, Sameen, Mou, and Mikey, for knowing every turn. Thank you, beyond all words, to my family, to Eva, and to all my dear ones, many of whom have come to know these poems intimately. And thank you above all to the Hara Kebira and the Hara Sgheira, for letting me in and not letting me in.

Djerba is located in the Gulf of Gabès, off the coast of Tunisia, and has an area of 510 square kilometers, with a population of just over a hundred thousand. There are a little more than one thousand Jews remaining on the island.

"Beginnings" was inspired by the violent beginning in the Enuma Elish, the Babylonian creation myth, as well as by a Native American creation myth.

"The Fall of the First Temple, 586 B.C.E., Jerusalem" is best contextualized through Djerban mourning rituals. Although mourning the Temple has been woven into the fabric of Judaism itself, its manifestations are acute in Djerba's Jewish community. A sugared wheat porridge (*basisa,* a symbol of the Temple's foundation) is stirred with a key (the Temple's lost key) once a year, acting out a longing to re-create the edifice. Older men wear black stripes on their trousers to mourn the Temple. A bride places a candle for mourning at her bedside. Two candelabra are painted on newly married couples' homes, making husband and wife into "pillars of the Temple to be rebuilt," as explained by Lucette Valensi, "Religious Orthodoxy or Local Tradition: Marriage Celebration in Southern Tunisia," in *Jews Among Arabs: Contacts and Boundaries,* ed. Mark Cohen and Abraham Udovitch (Princeton: Darwin Press, 1989).

In "Outside of Time" I make note of a preserved custom, unique to the Jews of Djerba, of blowing the ram's horn (shofar) to announce the arrival of the Sabbath.

"End of Time," "Outside of Time," "Ways to Be Redeemed," and indeed, the collection as a whole, are profoundly influenced by ideas of messianism within Judaism. Awaiting a Messiah to eliminate exile and usher in redemption has been integral to Judaism since the Second Temple period. According to Mircea Eliade, in *Myth of Eternal Return* (New York: Harper and Brothers, 1959), messianism seeks to "abolish history" (or more precisely, its grievances): "When the Messiah comes, the world will be saved once and for all and history will cease to exist." This sequence of events is imagined to occur in Israel; for Djerban Jews, with their profound messianism, Israel has long been intertwined with a mythical age to come. Jerusalem has been understood as the navel of the world, the emotional and imaginative core sustaining the larger Jewish community in Diaspora.

The collection as a whole is also deeply impacted by Zoharic thought. The Zohar offers a symbolic framework to think about exile, and then redemption. Djerban Jews, like many other Jews, believe the Zohar was composed in the second century by Rabbi Shimon Bar Yohai; in fact it was written in thirteenth-century Spain by Moses de Leon as a collection of Bar Yohai's lectures.

The Zohar elaborates a paradigm in which exile and redemption of the Jews become *cosmic* exile and redemption. The exile and redemption of God are even in the equation: in the unredeemed universe, God is exiled from God. Specifically, God is separated from and seeking reunion with the Shechinah, his female principle. By following ritual prescriptions, man can bring his community (and thus God) closer to redemption. Through prayer, he can help God and his Shechinah eventually reunite. Each individual thus has the power to impact the cosmos.

Although the Zohar's more esoteric ideas are likely understood only by a small group of scholars in Djerba, and not by the majority of the community, the book itself is nevertheless a ritual object laden with associations of great import. Placed at the center of messianic rituals, it is symbolically associated with Djerban Jewish ideas of final redemption.

Lurianic Kabbalah, an interpretation of Jewish mysticism developed by Isaac Luria (1534–72), is also critical to the work. Part of this extremely complex cosmology centers around a nexus of symbols called the shattering of the vessels. The vessel represents an all-encompassing unity or order; when it is shattered, exile, displacement, and grief come to the fore. Shards from the broken vessel—divine light—swirl through the cosmos. The vessels must be reassembled to begin repairing the torn cosmos. In Lurianic teachings, the act of prayer has been described as "lifting up the sparks" of one's own soul to, in turn, uplift the Shechinah (Gershon Scholem, *The Messianic Idea in Judaism and Other Essays on Jewish Spirituality* [London: Rushkin House, Schocken Books, 1971]). This act thereby helps to gather the shards into a whole.

Various strains of mysticism have percolated to Djerba. According to Ammiel Alcalay, "With the expulsion of the Jews from Spain in 1492 . . . [they were] welcomed with open arms by the Ottomans . . . The Zohar . . . that most unclassifiable of books, itself an amalgam of narrative, poetic and mystical conglomerate cutting through Christian Spain, infiltrated almost every aspect of the spiritual, communal and intellectual life of the Jewish Levant." Most Djerban Jews trace their origin to the Spanish expulsion; their Judaism is indeed inflected with the mystical messianic current that thrived thereafter. Moreover, in the seventeenth century, the Sabbatean messianic movement, which originated in what is now Turkey, was as strong in Morocco and Tunisia as in the Near East. Shabbetai Zvi's messianic movement triggered contact between North African communities and religious academies in Palestine. There are records of the presence of such emissaries in Djerba as early as the seventeenth century. One rabbi documents fifteen such visitors to Djerba's Jewish villages.

"Trapped on Djerba, Island of the Lotus Eaters" refers to the popular Djerban assumption that Homer was referring to Djerba in the myth. According to classical mythology, Odysseus nearly lost his men when they were fed the soporific lotus blossoms by the island's maidens; Djerba has since been called the island of forgetfulness. References to the myth now adorn hotels, spas, and casinos.

"Many Scientists Convert to Islam" was inspired by Søren Kierkegaard's *Fear and Trembling* and by an ongoing dialogue with a dear friend in Tunis.

I wrote the last section of this book in the Negev after a several-week stint interviewing Djerbans who had emigrated to Israel after 1948. This occurred during the Gaza withdrawal, a particularly fraught week, full of great hope for some and great despair for others. Most of my interviews were conducted in Netivot, Betigadi, Brechia, Tlamim, Ofakim, and Ashqelon. I also interviewed Djerbans in Lod, Tel Aviv, and Jerusalem. I came to each village or town with only a backpack and blank tapes and was offered hospitality by a different Djerban family every single night.

About the Author

Nomi Stone is a doctoral candidate in cultural anthropology at the Graduate Center of the City University of New York. Previously the assistant editor at the *Middle East Journal,* she has a master's degree in Middle Eastern studies from Oxford and was a Fulbright Scholar.